ECOSYSTEM FACTS THAT YOU SHOULD KNOW

THE SAVANNA AND TUNDRA

EDITION

Nature Picture Books | Children's Nature Books

BABY PROFESSOR
EDUCATION KIDS

Speedy Publishing LLC
40 E. Main St. #1156
Newark, DE 19711
www.speedypublishing.com

The savanna and the tundra never touch, but they have a lot in common. Read on and find out about these dry, but not desert, parts of the world.

Lonely elephant in the savanna.

WHAT IS THE SAVANNA?

A savanna is one of the two types of grassland, and is sometimes called tropical grassland. The other type is the temperate grassland that makes up areas like the Great Plains in the United States. For more about that type of grassland, read the Baby Professor book *Ecosystem Facts That You Should Know - The Desert and Grasslands Edition.*

The savanna is found closer to the equator, and often lies between a desert area and a tropical rain forest. It is rolling grassland with bushes and some trees here and there, but it seems very open and park-like. Savannas don't get enough rainfall to support a lot of trees.

Sunrise in savanna meadow in the mist with mountain background.

SAVANNA WEATHER

The savanna is pretty warm all through the year. It has a wet season and a long dry season.

When it is the dry season, there may be only a few inches of rain, or none at all. In the wet season, which is very hot, 15 or 25 inches of rain may fall each day. And the weather is so hot that moisture rises up from the ground and the damp ground-level air, meets cooler air above, turns into rain and falls again. Every summer day will see long afternoon rain storms.

Giraffes standing and eating from thorny bushes on the savanna.

LIFE ON THE SAVANNA

Typically, the wildlife on the savanna are a large number of herd animals, ranging from very small deer to elephants and giraffes, plus a much smaller number of animals like lions and leopards that hunt the herd animals. There is lots of bird life, including many birds that visit the savanna in the winter, while their homes further north are enduring much colder weather. Then they fly home in the spring.

To grow well in the savanna, plants have to have long, deep roots to get water from the ground, as many days may pass between rain storms. Grasses and small bushes burn quickly in bush fires, but return quickly. Larger plants like trees have thick bark to resist the heat and flames.

A lot of the grasses taste bitter so animals and bugs will leave them alone; some of them have very sharp edges to their leaves for the same reason.

Hamerkop (Scopus umbretta) on savanna, Masai Mara National Reserve, Kenya

But for every plant with a good defence, there is an animal who has learned to eat at least part of it. And for every herding animal, there is a hunter who will try to catch and eat the weakest, slowest, or most unlucky member of the herd.

As there are a lot of hawks and other birds of prey in the air, small animals tend to live in burrows. This keeps them safer from attack, and also lets them get out of the sun when it is hottest.

Two lionesses, Transvaal or Southeast African lion, resting in the green savanna. Timbavati game reserve, Kruger area, South Africa.

In Brazil, the savanna, or "cerrado", has many twisted trees that do not grow very high. The range of animals and plants is much broader than in many savannas around the world, and there are some creatures and plants here who do not exist anywhere else.

The caatinga landscape in Northeast Brazil

View on savanna plain with farmer fields. Lake Manyara National Park, Tanzania, Africa.

PRESSURE ON THE SAVANNA

People are very fond of taking parts of the savanna for farms or ranches, or to build houses and towns on. The land is flat, and it is much easier to create a farm or a village street there than it would be in the hills. Human occupation uses up more of the savanna every year.

Another problem is that farming and the climate of the savanna do not go all that well together. Savanna grasses are able to deal with drought, fires, and other threats, but plants that people farm need extra water and fertilizer to survive.

The grazing animals of the savanna eat a lot of the grass and shrubs, but then they move on and the plants have a chance to grow again. When people have cattle and sheep, they tend to put fences around them so they do not wander away or get stolen. The livestock eat the grasses in their enclosure until there is just bare ground, and they do not move away to let the ground recover.

Impala antelopes on the savanna in Africa.

When the grasses and bushes are under attack, it is easier for the desert to expand into the savanna. It is very hard to stop the desert, although countries in Africa are planting wide belts of trees to try to protect the savanna and people's farms and towns from the desert's invasion.

Crawshay's Zebras (Equus Quagga Crawshayi) in the South Luangwa Valley of Zambia, Africa.

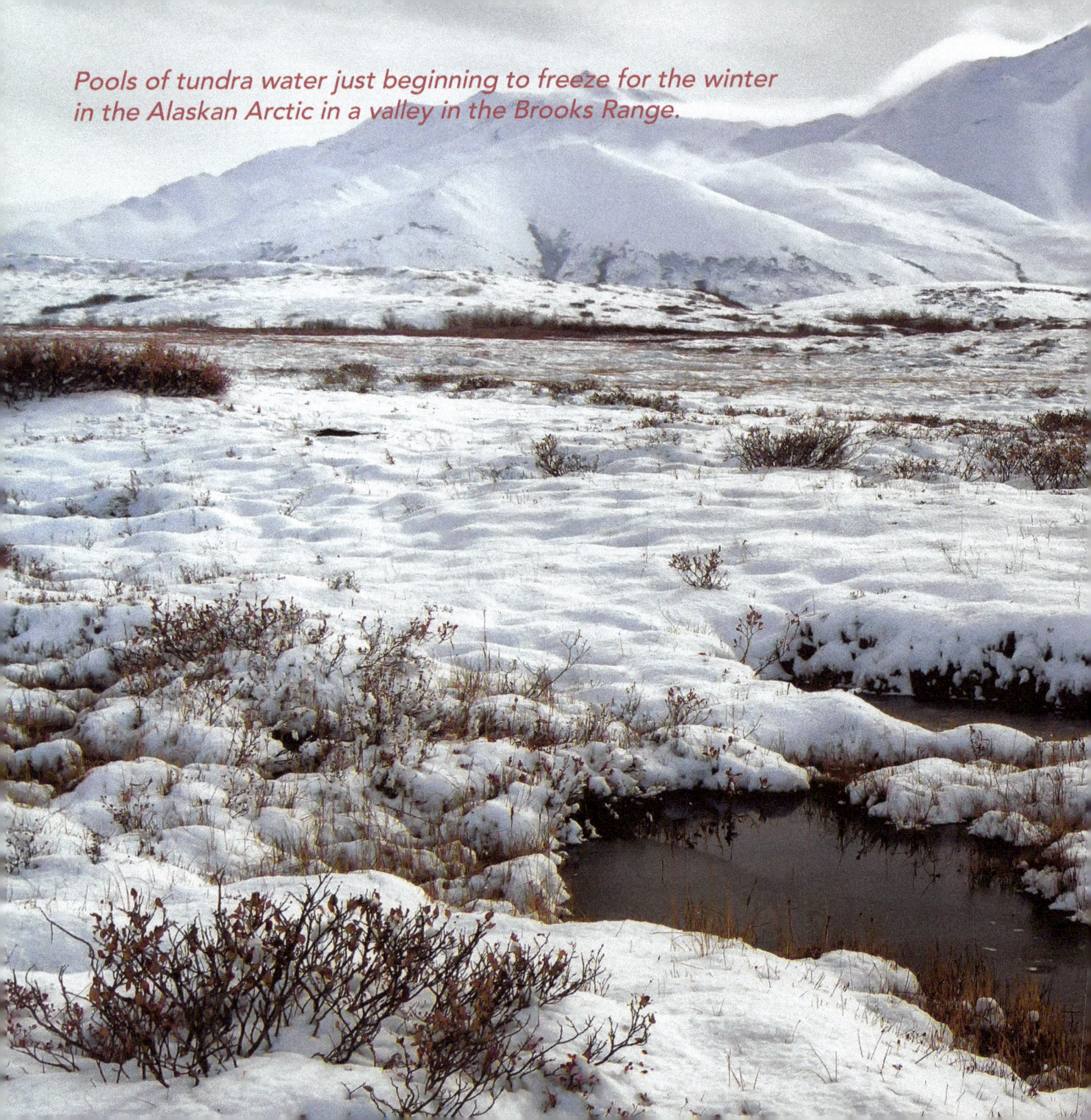

Pools of tundra water just beginning to freeze for the winter in the Alaskan Arctic in a valley in the Brooks Range.

WHAT IS THE TUNDRA?

The word "tundra" comes from "tunturia", a Finnish word that means "land that grows nothing." That is not quite accurate, but it is a hard place for plants and animals to call home.

The tundra is in the northern hemisphere, between 55 and 70 degrees north latitude. It goes all the way around the Earth, and covers about 20% of the dry land.

The tundra is quite cold, and as it has no trees it can look barren and lifeless—sort of a grey-green desert without sand or warmth.

TUNDRA
WEATHER

Spring and fall are very short periods in the tundra. The main seasons are a long, cold, dry winter and a much shorter summer.

Because the tundra is so far north, it has a huge change in the amount of daylight between summer and winter. In the summer, the sun may hardly set for days, while in the middle of winter you may only see the sun for an hour or two each day.

The tundra in the bloom with some kind of rhododendron.

The tundra tends to be quite dry, but huge winter storms can pick up any snow that has already fallen and send it tumbling through the air along with any new snow fall. Because there are no trees to slow it down, strong winds are almost a daily experience. Only six to ten inches of rain and (mostly) snow fall each year.

Alpine tundra

Pair of Gray wolfs (Canis lupus) in the tundra

TUNDRA LIFE

There may be no trees on the tundra, but if you look closely at the ground you will find a wide range of plants like mosses, heath, and lichen. These grow close to the ground to avoid the wind and the worst of the cold. They cannot set down deep roots because of the permafrost below.

The growing season each year is only about 60 days long, so plants don't get much of a chance to grow, put out flowers, get fertilized, make seeds, and prepare for the next generation.

Dusk on the tundra.

There are about fifty animal species that have their home in the tundra, which is not a wide range. They include small creatures like shrews, lemmings, and rodents; larger grazing animals like rabbits and deer; and hunters like bears, foxes, and wolves. Herds of caribou or reindeer move slowly across the land, eating plants and lichen and trying to stay out of the way of the fiercer animals.

There are lots of bird species, like ducks, geese, sandpipers, and plovers, who migrate south to more comfortable climates during the hardest part of the winter, and then come back with the warming spring.

A lot of the insect life does not migrate. In fact, mosquitoes have a kind of antifreeze in their bodies which keeps them from freezing while they wait under the snow for warmer weather. Then they quickly come out and start biting anything that moves!

Mountain Goats on the Tundra.

Norwegian Tundra.

THE CHANGING TUNDRA

A few inches below the surface of the tundra is the permafrost. This part of the Earth in the past never thawed, even in the height of summer. This meant that plants could not put down deep roots.

Now, with global warming, more and more of the permafrost is melting. This is changing the tundra landscape, as the surface of the land collapses and new lakes and bogs appear.

People move to the tundra to extract minerals from mines and oil from deep under the ground. The tundra is very fragile, and it does not recover well when huge trucks drive over it and vast machines generate a lot of heat. Human activity destroys the natural habitat for tundra wildlife, making their survival even harder.

Trans Alaska pipeline in the Tundra.

Many bird species travel north into the tundra, risking the poor weather because of the abundant insect life. But the more people move into the tundra, the more they use insecticides, drain the marshes and bogs, and do whatever else they can to get rid of the annoying insects. They may not realize they are also getting rid of what the birds need to eat!

Bewick's Swans and Mallard Ducks in the Tundra.

At first glance, it might seem like the tundra is not good for anything. But it is an essential part of our global environment. It is also very fragile. When humans treat the tundra the way they might treat more stable environments, the tundra suffers badly.

A WORLD WORTH KNOWING

You may never get to see the tundra, or visit herds of elephants walking across the savanna, but knowing where they live helps you understand and love our Earth more. Read other Baby Professor books, like *Who Lives in the Barren Desert?* and *What Every Child Should Know about Climate Change*, to learn even more.

Visit

BABY PROFESSOR
EDUCATION KIDS

www.BabyProfessorBooks.com

to download Free Baby Professor eBooks
and view our catalog of new and exciting
Children's Books

Lightning Source UK Ltd.
Milton Keynes UK
UKHW050808240420
362148UK00005B/46